Armed & Dangerous

Discovering Who You Are In God So That You Can Defeat The Enemy!

Shermaine Reed

Credits

Editors: Shanae St. Louis, Dorene Kittrell & Kiya Bonilla

Cover Designed by Dream Designs, Virginia Beach, Virginia

Interior Formatted by LaVon Featherstone

Foreword by Shanae St. Louis **www.shanaestlouis.com**

For permission requests, write to the publisher, addressed "Attention: Permissions Coordinator," at the address below.

Shermaine Reed International Ministries: **ssriministries@gmail.com**

Printed in the United States of America

Acknowledgements

*Every woman that has or is battling an identity crisis. May God's beauty shine through you & may His love and power break every chain that is keeping you in bondage. May you once and for all become **Armed & Dangerous**!*

It took me pressing and praying to release this book. The enemy did not want this book to be released so he fought me in every area of my life. I dedicate this book to my father, the King of ALL Kings, the restorer and redeemer of my life. The "I AM" in my life. It is through the power of God that I have become **Armed & Dangerous**.

To my husband Tyrene Reed, thank you for always pushing me and encouraging me to keep pressing through every obstacle. I love you always.

To my children Naielle, Tyra, Abbygail and Xavier may you always S.T.E.P (Stand Tall Encompassing Power), mommy love you always.

To my mother Martha and my sister Christie, you have both kept me smiling and uplifted through some difficult times, I love you my ladies.

To my editors and sisters Kiya Bonilla, Shanae St. Louis and Dorene Kittrell, thank you very much for your hard work.

My sister and prayer warrior Shanae St. Louis you are a phenomenal woman of God your faith has strengthened mine.

To my Co-Pastor Sharon Crest, you gave me encouragement to walk into my destiny and to unleash the woman of power that is inside of me. You took me from jeans and sneakers to high heels and dresses. I thank God for the second mother I have found in you.

To my Pastor, William Crest, thank you for being a father figure in my life. I praise God for you.

To my adopted baby sister Quenisha Kittrell, I pray you begin to see what I see and what God has placed in you. You are a beautiful woman of God and there is a bright future in store for you. Let go of your fears and walk into your destiny.

To my father, Colin Nicholas, I love you and thank God for you.

To my grandmother Angie Nicholas, you are an inspiration to me. I watched you press towards God after the death of my grandfather with such amazing strength and passion. I love you my gran.

To my grandfather, Victor Nicholas, I miss you dearly.

Contents

Embrace the process and
Let the journey begin!

"For what profit is it to a man if he gains the whole world, and loses his own soul? Or what will a man give in exchange for his soul?"

Matthew 16:26(NKJV)

"Behold, I give you the authority to trample on serpents and scorpions, and over all the power of the enemy, and nothing shall by any means hurt you."

Luke 10:19 (NKJV)

"I will praise You, for I am fearfully and wonderfully made; Marvelous are Your works, And that my soul knows very well."

Psalm 139:14 (NKJV)

Foreword

By *Shanae St. Louis*

Who am I? What am I doing here? Why me? Why not me? So many questions! One true answer, yet so many women struggle with poor self-image and no idea of their true identity. How they see themselves because of failures in relationships, education, career goals, body image and so much more has distorted what God the Creator of all things had originally designed. But the truths found in this book will devastate the plans of the enemy of your destiny and set all of those who read it on the path to demolishing the myths and empower them to arm themselves with the infallible word of God which makes them exceptionally dangerous to the works of our adversary and even our own flesh. Shermaine Reed's first book "More Than A Conqueror" gave such a vivid testimony to the healing and restoration power of the LORD as she shared how she overcame her past but "Armed& Dangerous" goes to another place as it attempts to warn us of the tricks of the enemy, encourages us to seek God to realize who we are and then charges us to walk boldly and confidently, knowing our worth, as the Woman of God we were created to be.

What I love about this influential tool is each insightful step that she lays out is a like a road map to follow as we discover the warrior God has called us to be. If we take this journey toward our own personal greatness, in connection to GOD, by the time you finish the last page of the book you will feel motivated to take one quick look back to where you were and with a running start you know that you can leap into the destiny God has already purposed and ordained.

So much of this book is written from the author's life experiences and therefore encourages the reader to trust God to heal, deliver, encourage, and empower them as well.

I can recall reading an early manuscript of "Armed& Dangerous" at my desk and thinking many lives will be elevated in places once thought impossible because of the revelation that will take place once they realize the power that lies within them. Once they embrace and love the person God created and sees daily, there will be no area in their lives that they cannot conqueror. Shermaine shares with us very powerfully how God created us with loving purpose and that He offers us his unconditional acceptance; we need only receive it. Once we receive it and make up in our minds that we should not accept anything less from others, then how we view ourselves and how others view us changes for the better. That's what being armed is, it is having the knowledge of the truth that we are fearfully and wonderfully made, that before the foundations of the world God had a plan to prosper us , give us hope and a future, and that according to His word we can do ALL things through Christ who gives us strength. The enemy doesn't want us to know these truths and often uses our past failings and personal insecurities against us to keep us from growing and moving forward. Once armed with the Sword of the Spirit we become extremely dangerous to any and everything that attempts to pervert or destroy what God has already called us to be.

This book serves as a God inspired wake up call to any woman who has doubted who they are. Once we embrace who we are and whose we are, we take the weapons of fear and doubt out of the hands of our enemies and equip ourselves with power and confidence through God.

Introduction

You might be wondering to yourself, what does it mean to be Armed & Dangerous? I'll tell you what it does not mean. Armed & Dangerous does not mean for you to go out and purchase a 9mm to strap to your hips when you leave your house. NO! Armed & Dangerous is a movement! It is overcoming identity crisis, low self-esteem, insecurities and every label that the world has placed on you. It is, standing tall refusing to live your life as a victim. It is, being confident in who you are as a woman and who God has called you to be. It is, being real with yourself and loving "YOU" inside and out.

When you become Armed & Dangerous, you are no longer slave to Satan and his demons. You become Armed & Dangerous by being real with yourself in regards to where you are in life and by allowing God to break every chain, bondage, and every yoke and uprooting them from your life. It is through the word of God and by putting on the complete, full armor of God that you become Armed & Dangerous. God created you with divine purpose. You are beautiful inside and out.

Often times as women, we look to others to define who we are as a woman, and child of God. My hearts cry and reason for writing this book is to empower women to stand tall and embrace the power and authority God has given them. I want to see every woman, around the world being bold, embracing her true beauty and living victorious lives. It is through a personal relationship with Christ that you will be set free.

God took me through a transformation, where I had to learn to be confident in who I am and who He has called ME to be. I was so lost and deeply wounded from my past, that I lost the sense of being a woman. I was a woman bound in shame and guilt. It was evident through my facial expressions, and posture. I felt unworthy of love, and it affected every area of my life especially my marriage. I felt I wasn't beautiful enough to wear dresses or heels because I felt I had no power, beauty or purpose. God took me through a breaking season and uprooted every tormenting, belittling, oppressive spirit that was keeping me from fulfilling my destiny. The transformation was so profound that today, I stand tall unashamed with power, in my heels, dresses and afro hair, free to be me and who God has called me to be.

When you are Armed & Dangerous, you become unstoppable, unmovable, and unshakeable. You become a threat to the enemy. If the enemy is not afraid of you, you are not walking in the power that's inside of you. When you are Armed & Dangerous, you will be able to overcome every situation you face with peace, wisdom and BOLDNESS. Your faith will SILENCE every fear that dare rise up in your mind. The enemy will not be able to stop you. Can you imagine a world where every woman is Armed & Dangerous with the word of God and operating in their God given gifts? My God! When you become Armed & Dangerous, you become a chain breaker. You become a trailblazer. A GAMECHANGER! You bring forth change to generations by walking in AUTHORITY and PURPOSE. God uses women bring forth change. He used Deborah who was a woman of courage and great faith in God. She was a leader that led with wisdom.

When faced with a David and Goliath situation, she led the out-numbered and badly-equipped Israelite troops to a great victory. She was referred to as the "mother of Israel" because of her leadership in the battle against the Canaanites. Deborah was obedient to the word of God and allowed her faith to rise up in her to FULFILL what God called HER to do. She was confident in who she was as a woman, a wife, and a leader. She was confident in who she was in God. In order to walk in your purpose, you must be confident in who you are as a child of God and as the leader you are called to be. God says in His word that He has given you DOMINION POWER!

The days of you being the devils punching bag are over. It is time for you to **CHANGE THE GAME!** It is time for **YOU** to become "**Armed & Dangerous!**"

There is greatness inside of you! It is time for the birthing process to take place. Embrace your true identity and allow God to transform YOU!

Chapter 1
Identity Crisis

Chapter 1

Identity Crisis

Too many women are walking around looking like beautiful question marks dressed in makeup, nice hair and pumps, not knowing the real person on the inside.

Are you unsure of your purpose in life? Do you ever feel like you don't know the real you? Do you often find yourself asking the questions: Who am I? Why am I here? Or why me?

Many women suffer with identity crises, causing them to forfeit their true purpose and destiny. According to the Collins Dictionary the word identity is defined as "the condition or fact of being a specific person or thing; individuality". The Collins Dictionary defined the word crisis as "a turning point in the course of anything; decisive or crucial time, stage, or event". When God created you, He didn't create anyone else like you. You are one of a kind. You are unique. You are a beautiful treasure. There is an assignment on your life that only you can fulfill. There is only one authentic you. We live in a world where too many women are lost.

There are women in the world who are confused about their sexuality. Our society has accepted homosexuality as the new thing and our young ladies are grabbing hold of the confusion they are being fed. The devil is on a rampage to destroy the power and voice in women. Women in the workplace, church, school and homes are being oppressed with the thought that they simply do not fit in where they are. We live in a world where many are searching for a sense of belonging to someone or something. Our sisters are suffering from a state of identity crisis and are walking around dazed, lost and confused. Yes I said our sisters, we are all called to be brothers and sisters in Christ. We are supposed to be held accountable for each other. But are we? Are you your sister's keeper?

God did not create you to exist. You were designed with purpose, built with an impenetrable armor and birthed with destiny.

The images of women in today's society, is continually being repackaged to appeal to her insecurities, sense of worthlessness, and covert or overt desire for power. Hollywood has created a false identity of what a real woman is to be. Today, regardless of what time you turn on the television, there are commercials and shows that belittle a woman's worth. Yet many women are striving to achieve this false sense of womanhood with hopes to fill a void in their lives. Commercials promoting alcoholic drinks feature women wearing long, slim fitting, sexy gowns, makeup and high heels, while smiling and laughing.

These women are portrayed as being strong, bold and secure in who they are from having these drinks. They are viewed as being filled with joy. Commercials such as this contribute to the rise of alcoholism and drug addiction amongst women. Many women are being drawn to this false sense of being confident and beautiful. Many develop a deep sense of desire for the identities of the women seen in the commercials. For this reason, it is imperative that those who comprise the Body of Christ give serious attention to the ways women are being misrepresented. We must acknowledge that the beauty in which God created women is being distorted. It is our responsibility as the body of Christ to stand up and be a voice for those that are weak. We should not stand by and watch our sisters falling and living a life of defeat, failure and bound in chains. We should be our sisters' keeper!

Girls are born with two eyes, legs, arms, ears, lips and other important body parts. Her parents oftentimes choose her name before her birth. She grows up believing that name they gave her at birth is her identity. Often times when you ask a woman the question "Who are you?" she will give you her birth name. As time goes by she transforms from a daughter into a woman, a girlfriend, a wife, and a mother. The transformation process may cause her to continually lose her real identity and turn into a fake, vulnerable and dependent woman with nothing of her own. Teenagers spend their high school years in search of their true identity. They join different school clubs such as the debate team and cheerleading in search of a purpose.

The transition from high school to college can become overwhelming and confusing stage in life for many. When speaking to their guidance counselor they are asked the question, "What do you want to be?" They are not asked, "What has God called you or predestined you to be?" The road to the identity crisis continued from there.

Picture yourself at a women's conference, what would you do if the speaker asked the following question : "How many of you have incurred debt from going to college and switching majors over and over in search of who you want to be?" I don't know about you, but I would have both hands and a foot raised because that's where I was. I spent years going into debt in search of "me" and what "I" wanted to be. The fact that God has a great purpose and destiny for my life was never shared with me. I searched through different professions and instead of living a life of prosperity, I adapted a poverty mentality. A poverty mentality will have you thinking that all you need is a job to be able to pay your bills. There is no hope for financial freedom with a poverty mentality. With that mind frame, you end up settling for less and expecting nothing more. Seeking after an identity that is driven by self will cause you to miss your blessings. There will be no peace and security in your life when operating in self. God has great things for His children, His plan is that you prosper in all things.

"Beloved, I pray that you may prosper in all things and be in health, just as your soul prospers." 3 John 1:2 (NKJV)

*You will find peace and security when you
stop functioning in self-mode and choose to
operate in Gods mode.*

Selfish ambitions leads to false identity.

There is a great need for a united voice amongst Christian women and a desperate cry for change. It is time for us as women to bond together and uplift each other. It is crucial that the term no man left behind be adopted amongst us. We should be chanting "No woman left behind!"

According to advertisings and media marketing in the society in which we live, there is no such thing as a real woman. The image of what a woman is supposed to look like, changes from magazine to magazine and television shows. Women are being labeled as sex objects. As a woman it is important to set high standards for yourself. You should never allow yourself to be viewed as just an image of sex nor should you accept such a status in your relationship. There is a quote by Alexander Hamilton that says, "He who stands for nothing will fall for anything." If you do not know who you are, you will believe anything that is told to you. You will end up believing the labels that people put on you such as ugly, dark skin, the B word, big eyes, big lips, fat and many more.

Today, young women are walking around proudly accepting other people call them "my B****".

They allow young men to call them that, and it brings a smile to their faces from here to Timbuktu. In their minds, being called a "B****" means the guy likes them. The term "B****" refers to a female dog. A female dog when she vomits, eats her own vomit, and that's what young women are accepting as a standard for themselves. Somewhere along the line mothers, we failed our daughters and they lost the status of being "Women of Standard". Labels placed on you that you accept and believe, will cause you to fall into a state of depression and be subject to anxiety attacks. Labels bring on self-doubt and low self-esteem.

If you do not know who God has called and predestined you to be, you will become vulnerable and believe anything that is told to you by men that come into your life.

You are more than the weave you put on your head or the clothes on your back. You are more than the makeup that paints your face. You do not have to cover up who you are to succumb to anyone's expectations of who you are supposed to be. How many hair weaves have you been through as a woman? Now don't get me wrong, there is nothing wrong with hair weaves. However, when you wear the weave to put on an identity that is not yours, to cover up pain, guilt, shame and to keep the person God has designed you to be concealed, then that is not just wrong it is spiritual suicide. You are aborting the woman in you and walking around simply existing in a false identity. In spite of what the world thinks you are and the labels others place on you, it is important to know who God says you are.

God calls you the apple of His eyes, a royal priesthood.

You were bought with a price, you are not a product of yourself. In order to learn who you are, you have to turn to God, the One who made you in such a beautiful, unique and perfect design.

"But you are a chosen generation, a royal priesthood, a holy nation, His own special people, that you may proclaim the praises of Him who called you out of darkness into His marvelous light;" 1 Peter 2:9 (NKJV)

"Or do you not know that your body is the temple of the Holy Spirit who is in you, whom you have from God, and you are not your own? For you were bought at a price; therefore glorify God in your body[a] and in your spirit, which are God's." 1 Corinthians 6:19-20 (NKJV)

You are a priceless treasure!

Affirmation #1

I AM a BEAUTIFUL child of GOD!

I AM who GOD says I am!

I AM FEARFULLY and WONDERFULLY made!

Chapter 2

Overcoming Identity Crisis

Chapter 2

Overcoming Identity Crisis

One of the greatest keys to unlock your identity is to learn who you are in Christ. God shows us that women are unique, possessing great power and influence, and having value far beyond looks or aspirations. The Bible teaches us stories of women who were great warriors. Women who when they fasted and prayed, generations were changed. Women of great character and faith. The Bible speaks highly of women of character and value.

A Wife of Noble Character

"Who can find a virtuous and capable wife? She is more precious than rubies. Her husband can trust her, and she will greatly enrich his life. She brings him good, not harm, all the days of her life. She finds wool and flax and busily spins it. She is like a merchant's ship, bringing her food from afar. She gets up before dawn to prepare breakfast for her household and plan the day's work for her servant girls. She goes to inspect a field and buys it; with her earnings she plants a vineyard. She is energetic and strong, a hard worker. She makes sure her dealings are profitable; her lamp burns late into the night. Her hands are busy spinning thread, her fingers twisting fiber. She extends a helping hand to the poor and opens her arms to the needy. She has no fear of winter for her household, for everyone has warm clothes. She makes her own bedspreads. She dresses in fine linen and purple gowns.

Her husband is well known at the city gates, where he sits with the other civic leaders. She makes belted linen garments and sashes to sell to the merchants. She is clothed with strength and dignity, and she laughs without fear of the future. When she speaks, her words are wise, and she gives instructions with kindness. She carefully watches everything in her household and suffers nothing from laziness. Her children stand and bless her. Her husband praises her: "There are many virtuous and capable women in the world, but you surpass them all!" Charm is deceptive, and beauty does not last; but a woman who fears the Lord will be greatly praised. Reward her for all she has done. Let her deeds publicly declare her praise." Proverbs 31:10-31 New Living Translation (NLT)

Verse 25 says, "She is clothed with strength and dignity, and she laughs without fear of the future". Life will throw many different obstacles at you that will test your faith, character and very existence. It is important to understand that the trials you face today, will position you for receiving your greater tomorrow. Trials come to build you up in your faith, power and love of God. When trials come, stand strong and let God be God in your life.

When Pharaohs army was pursuing the Israelites, God parted the Red Sea for them to be able to walk through it on dry land. Now if God can divide the sea and cause them to walk on dry land, He can surely mend your broken heart, pay your bills, deliver your children, save your marriage, heal your family and be everything that you need Him to be in your life.

There is no limit to what God can do. The limit exist in your mind, that's why the word of God instructs us, to renew our minds that we may prove the perfect will of God for our lives. When you change the way you think, your attitude will shift in the midst of trials. A positive attitude will allow you to stand with peace, knowing that God is in control of the outcome. There is nothing too hard for God to do!

"Now to Him who is able to do exceedingly abundantly above all that we ask or think, according to the power that works in us," Ephesians 3:20 (NKJV)

"And do not be conformed to this world, but be transformed by the renewing of your mind, that you may prove what is that good and acceptable and perfect will of God." Romans 12:2 (NKJV)

For years I struggled with my identity but I am a living testimony that God can and will restore you, if you let Him. Not only has God delivered me from MANY things, He has totally transformed my life. My lips shall forever sing of His greatness. I want to see every woman of God walking in authority and power. It is your inheritance, embrace it! Claim it! Receive it!

"For you are a holy people to the Lord your God; the Lord your God has chosen you to be a people for Himself, a special treasure above all the peoples on the face of the earth." Deuteronomy 7:6 (NKJV)

There are four important key steps to follow in order to overcome an identity crisis.

- Know Your Enemy
- Put on the complete and full armor of God
- Overcome fear
- See yourself through the eyes of God

Before you move on to these key steps, I want you to take a moment and reflect on the word of God. You have what it takes on the inside of you to overcome the sin and distractions in your life. You can make it through that very thing the enemy is trying to use to kill you. You have power over the enemy, command your spirit to rise up and activate! The victory is already yours. God won the battle for you!

"I can do all things through Christ who strengthens me." Philippians 4:13(NKJV)

Before you begin to study the four key steps to overcoming Identity Crisis, pray this prayer of protection. The enemy does not want you to overcome your past and become empowered. Arm yourself in prayer. There is POWER in PRAYER!

Prayer:

I decree and declare that as I continue on the journey to overcoming Identity crisis, the scales will begin to fall from my eyes. I declare right now in the name of Jesus that the love of God will fall strongly on me and wrap me in His arms. I speak to the very pain that I have been hiding from everyone and command healing to take place right now in the mighty name of Jesus. I command these dried bones to come alive. I declare a shift in the atmosphere and new life shall spring forth. I decree and declare that the tricks of the enemy shall no longer work in my life. Lord I command your Angels to build a hedge of protection around me as I journey into the next phase of this book and my life. I thank you for victory right now in Jesus name, Amen.

Affirmation #2

I AM an OVERCOMER!

I have POWER inside of me that can bring forth CHANGE!

I AM MORE THAN a CONQUEROR!

Chapter 3

Know Your Enemy

Chapter 3

Know Your Enemy

"In the beginning God created the heavens and the earth." Genesis 1:1 (NKJV)

It is important to know that Satan did not create anything or anyone, therefore he cannot destroy you!

"He has delivered us from the power of darkness and conveyed us into the kingdom of the Son of His love," Colossians 1:13(NKJV)

Your enemy is not the woman in the store who cut in front of you at the register. It is not your best friend who stabbed you in the back. It is not your father who never loved you and wanted to acknowledge you as his child. It is not another human being. Your enemy is Satan the Devil, AKA, Lucifer, Abaddon (Destruction), Adversary, the Evil One, the Enemy, Murderer, Liar, Ruler of Darkness, Apollyon (Destroyer), Dragon, Accuser of the brethren, Deceiver. He is the prince of the power of the air and the accuser of our brethren. He is in direct opposition of everything that God is working to fulfill. He is an imposter and an impersonator.

It is important to know the voice of God, so when Satan talks to you, you can defend yourself. When Satan talks, he plants seeds of doubt, fear, discord and thoughts that goes against the word of God. Satan is intelligent, don't be fooled.

It is through his intelligence that he was able to deceive Adam and Eve in the Garden of Eden. His deception caused them to give up their position to rule over the world. However, Satan's powers are not limitless. His power is subject to Gods restrictions. Satan had to ask God for permission to afflict Job. Though he is permitted to afflict Gods people, he is never permitted to win an ultimate victory over them. The purpose of your afflictions, is for you to grow stronger in your faith and anointing.

Satan uses many methods to carry out his evil work but his greatest one is TEMPTATION. Have you ever found yourself in a place where you were plagued with loneliness, grief or emptiness and felt the need to fill the void that weighed heavy inside of you? It is at your weakest point that Satan will try to tempt you and cause you to step off the path God has placed you on. Satan tried to tempt Jesus in the book of Matthew during his time of weakness to turn the stones into bread. Satan will exploit your weakness. He will try to lead you to compromise your walk in God by promising you things that God has already given you. It is important to wait on the Lord and know the promises of God for your life. Do not move ahead of God or you will be out of Gods will. Satan is an expert at falsifying the truth.

Satan rules over the kingdom of darkness. The word of God tells us that God has already delivered us from darkness. Jesus died on the cross for our sins and rose with ALL power in His hand. When God created man, he gave man dominion over everything on the earth. YOU have the power and authority over the enemy!

"Behold, I give you the authority to trample on serpents and scorpions, and over all the power of the enemy, and nothing shall by any means hurt you." Luke 10:19 NKJV

"Then God blessed them, and God said to them, "Be fruitful and multiply; fill the earth and subdue it; have dominion over the fish of the sea, over the birds of the air, and over every living thing that moves on the earth." Genesis 1:28(NKJV)

Seek to glorify God each day with your life. Anything in your life that offends God, uproot it and fill that space with the word of God. God gave you authority to trample over the enemy, it is up to you to execute that authority. Satan seeks to be a god in the lives of God's people. James 4:7 teaches us to submit to God and resist the devil. All it takes is one word from God and Satan and his army will cease to exist in your life. There is no need to fear Satan because God has built a hedge of protection around you that is impenetrable, when you are in Gods will. Notice I said when you are in Gods will, when you are operating outside the will of God, you open doors for the enemy to get in and have his way in your life. God has not left you defenseless against Satan, He sent His only begotten son Jesus Christ, who has risen with all power and overcame sin and death.

"Therefore submit to God. Resist the devil and he will flee from you." James 4:7(NKJV)

"Having disarmed principalities and powers, He made a public spectacle of them, triumphing over them in it." Colossians 2:15 (NKJV)

Satan loves to attack you when you are weak. Have you ever found yourself in a place where it seems like everything just kept going wrong? Have you ever asked yourself, what else can go wrong? That's one of the tricks of the enemy, to beat you down when you are already down. His plan is to get you so low that you cannot get back up. If you are in a place that seems impossible and everywhere you turn, opposition is on every side, know that God will reach into the darkest of dark places to pull you out. You might be tangled in the sin of homosexuality, prostitution, adultery, cheating or fornication, whatever your sin is, God can and will deliver you if you turn to Him and cry out to Him for forgiveness and mercy. Take it from someone that has been there. I remember sitting on my bed one night crying out to God feeling so ashamed and dirty. I heard the voice of Satan say, He won't take you back look how far out you are, look at what you just did, you are married, you don't deserve love, he was trying to take my life by planting the seed of suicide in my mind. SUDDENLY, it was as if time stopped. I heard a sweet gentle voice say, "Even now, I am still here".

I want you to know that no matter where you are in life, God is saying to you, "Even now, I am still here". His word says, He would never leave you nor forsake you. If I listened to the voice of Satan that night, I would not be writing this book. I would not have birthed my international ministry, through which many lives are being empowered and transformed. Satan attacks you to try and stop you from fulfilling your purpose and destiny. Know the enemy for who he is, know his tactics and begin to fight back with the power God has placed inside of you.

The word of God teaches us not to love the world. The enemy will use the lust of the flesh, the lust of the eyes and the pride of life to tempt you and cause you to fall.

The spirit and flesh are in a constant daily battle between the lust of the flesh, the lust of the eyes, and the pride of life. The lust of the flesh is the lust of the body. It is true that our bodies have needs for food, for drink, for touch, for intimacy, for healing, and many other things. The problem is not that the body has wants and needs, but that it falls prey to lusting for them. **Lust is not love, it is a craving for what is forbidden rather than for what is allowed.** Love is a wholesome desire, lust is a perverted one. Lust seeks sex outside of marriage, food in excess, healing through new age practices, it goes against the word of God. The devil seeks to trick us to fulfill these desires through the wrong things. God gave us eyes to see the wonders of His creative genius and to take in information to help us to spiritually discern and make decisions. Our ability to see is a gift from God, but Satan deceives us up by causing us to use our eyes to lust.

The world knows how to use lust to market things to us by doing lavish presentations in store windows and flashy lights at a casino. There is a reason why sex sells. Satan will use anything he can to cause you to fall. That is his "A" game. Tap into your power and develop your "A" game. Do not become a casualty of war. **Be in it to WIN it!**

"Do not love the world or the things in the world. If anyone loves the world, the love of the Father is not in him. For all that is in the world— the lust of the flesh, the lust of the eyes, and the pride of life—is not of the Father but is of the world." 1 John 2:15-16(NKJV)

"Be strong and of good courage, do not fear nor be afraid of them; for the Lord your God, He is the One who goes with you. He will not leave you nor forsake you." Deuteronomy 31:6(NKJV)

Affirmation #3

I have POWER over Satan's schemes!

I am a VICTOR not a victim!

I will STAND in GODs WILL!

Chapter 4

How to Overcome Fear

Chapter 4

How to Overcome Fear

The Collins dictionary defines fear as an emotion induced by a perceived threat, which causes entities to quickly pull far away from it and usually hide. My definition of fear is:

Fear is an emotion induced in your mind by the enemy to cause YOU relinquish all your rights to your purpose, destiny and blessing.

2 Timothy 1:7 NLT says "For God has not given us a spirit of fear and timidity, but of power, love and self-discipline."

Fear is something that many battle with; it's the enemy's way of distracting you and taking you off course. It is a spirit sent by Satan to attack your peace, courage, vision and faith. It has the power to cause you to abort the very purpose God has placed in you, and cause you to miss your destiny. God has not given you the spirit of fear. When fear tries to attack you, declare the word of God over your mind.

"You shall not be afraid of the terror by night, Nor of the arrow that flies by day," Psalm 91:5(NKJV)

"For God has not given us a spirit of fear, but of power and of love and of a sound mind." 2 Timothy 1:7(NKJV)

Verse 25 of Proverbs 31 tells us, "She laughs without fear of the future." That is a woman who is confident not only in who she is but also in who God says she is. She must be confident in the God that lives in her and holds her life in the palm of His hands. She might be faced with eviction, divorce, death, failure, hunger, and many other trials and tribulations but because of her faith in God she laughs and smiles with confidence knowing that her future is secured in God.

You must come to place, where you are unshakeable and unmovable by the circumstances that surround you.

Fear and Faith cannot coexist.

In order to overcome fear you must be armed with God's word at all times. God gave us the most powerful weapon you could ever have to conqueror and annihilate the attacks of the enemy. The marine's weapon of choice is the rifle, which they use in war. God has given you His word! The word of God is mighty in battle and will calm every storm. I am not saying things will change in the twinkling of an eye, what I am saying is that even thou you might be going through, you will have peace, joy and hope. It is in the word of God that you can find strength to conqueror every battle. The word of God in Romans 8:37 teaches us that we are More Than Conquerors. Not just an ordinary conqueror but More Than!

To conqueror, you have to go into battle. You have to fight. You cannot be afraid to step into the ring! To be more than a conqueror means that before you ever get a problem, you are confident in the fact that God promises to bring you out victoriously. God loves you no matter what and He will never leave you nor forsake you. When unexpected things happens or you're disappointed, you won't be devastated, because you know who you are and whose you are.

When you walk in fear, Satan can confuse you and keep you from your victory. Remember the enemy wants to kill, steal and destroy what God has for you.

Hebrews 4:12 NLT says, "For the word of God is alive and powerful. It is sharper than the sharpest two-edged sword, cutting between soul and spirit, between joint and marrow. It exposes our innermost thoughts and desires."

"Be anxious for nothing, but in everything by prayer and supplication, with thanksgiving, let your requests be made known to God; and the peace of God, which surpasses all understanding, will guard your hearts and minds through Christ Jesus." Philippians 4:6-7 (NKJV)

The key to overcoming fear, is to have total and complete trust in God. When you trust God, you are boldly serving the enemy notice and letting him know that you refuse to give in to fear. It is turning to God even in the darkest times and trusting Him to cause a shift in your situation. You might be facing eviction, terminal illness, overdue bills or any other catastrophic situations that to your natural eyes might seem impossible to overcome. Trust God to bring you out of it all.

Do not be overtaken by fear. Job when faced with one of the most difficult situation in life said, "Though he slay me, yet will I trust in him" (Job 13:15 NKJV). Trust in God no matter what it may look like. It was trust in God that gave David the courage and power to defeat Goliath. There may be giants in your life that you have been afraid to face. Don't look at the giants in your life, look at your God and the mighty demon destroying weapon He has placed in your hands. You have the power within you to overcome. You have the power within you to get back up. You have the power within you to fight this race and WIN! You are victorious. No longer shall fear be in your vocabulary. Trust God to be the "I AM" in your life.

Don't allow your past to cripple your growth and block your purpose. Seek God and watch what your pain produce.

In order to succeed you must overcome the fear of failure.

The God of your future is stronger than the enemy of your past.

Affirmation #4

I AM BOLD!

I AM COURAGEOUS!

I AM FEARLESS!

Chapter 5

Put on the

"Complete", Full

Armor of God

Chapter 5

Put on the "Complete"

Full Armor of God

With God's word, you remain equipped for war. Not only did God give you His word as a weapon but He also gave you instructions on how to prepare for war. God instructs you in His word, to put on the whole armor of God. Not parts of it but the WHOLE ARMOR. How many times have you gotten dressed and decided not to put a belt on your jeans saying to yourself, "Oh, I don't need it today, these jeans fit me just fine" only to find yourself constantly pulling them up to avoid your underwear from showing? The same way you need to make sure you are fully dressed and prepared to step outside, is the same way you need to make sure you are fully clothed and prepared for spiritual warfare. You don't need to save up money or max out credit cards to try and buy armor. You don't need layaway. The only thing you need to lay away is your "self". God has freely given you His armor; all you have to do is choose to accept it, pick it up and put it on. In order to overcome Identity Crisis you must put on the complete armor of God.

"Finally, my brethren, be strong in the Lord and in the power of His might. Put on the whole armor of God, that you may be able to stand against the wiles of the devil. For we do not wrestle against flesh and blood, but against principalities, against powers, against the rulers of the darkness of this age, against spiritual hosts of wickedness in the heavenly places.

Therefore take up the whole armor of God, that you may be able to withstand in the evil day, and having done all, to stand. Stand therefore, having girded your waist with truth, having put on the breastplate of righteousness, and having shod your feet with the preparation of the gospel of peace; above all, taking the shield of faith with which you will be able to quench all the fiery darts of the wicked one. And take the helmet of salvation, and the sword of the Spirit, which is the word of God; praying always with all prayer and supplication in the Spirit, being watchful to this end with all perseverance and supplication for all the saints-" Ephesians 6:10-18 (NKJV)

The armor of God equips you with the power you need to defeat the enemy. It is a solid protection against the weapons of the enemy. The enemy seeks to destroy your identity, to keep you from maximizing your God given potential and stop you from fulfilling your destiny. Although our armor might be invisible to the naked eye, that does not mean it is powerless.

"For though we in the flesh, we do not war according to the flesh. For the weapons of our warfare are not carnal but mighty in God for the pulling down of strongholds," 2 Corinthians 10:3-4 NKJV

You can see a great example, of the importance of having on the Armor of God in one of my favorite books of the Bible, the book of Matthew.

"Then Jesus was led up by the Spirit into the wilderness to be tempted by the devil. And when he had fasted forty days and forty nights, afterward He was hungry. Now when the tempter came to Him, he said, "If you are the Son of God, command that these stones become bread." But He answered and said, "It is written, man shall not live by bread alone, but by every word that proceeds from the mouth of God." Matthew 4:1-4 NKJV

In verse 3, we see the enemy testing Jesus by commanding Him to turn the stones to bread. So basically the enemy was telling Him to prove himself. He was saying show me! What are you going to do?! You not about that life, what you got?

What the enemy didn't realize, is that Jesus had no need to question who He was. Someone could ask you right now to prove yourself, saying, "No you are lying, I want proof, let me see it." As humans our first instinct is to prove ourselves. Often times, we get into such a rush to do so that we end up looking foolish. As soon as we make attempts to prove who we are, we end up messing up and then questioning our own abilities, "well maybe I'm not who I think I am, maybe I'm not good enough." See, the enemy will use people to get to you and cause you to doubt who you are as well as your potential. That is the greatest and oldest trick of the enemy. The enemy wants you to doubt yourself because he does not want you to get to your destiny. That is why it is very important to watch who you keep in your circle.

Not everyone who is around you is for you.

As a woman of God and a visionary, I had to learn for myself that the greatest friend I can have is Jesus. One of the greatest things you can ever do in life is free yourself from people. People will bring you down and will doubt your ability to carry out the vision God has given you. When you are confident in who you are in Christ, you do not need to prove yourself to anyone. I am not saying for you to live life without friends, what I am saying is be very careful of who you choose to call your friend and share your vision with.

"Fearing people is a dangerous trap, but trusting the Lord means safety." Proverbs 29:25 NLT

You cannot please everybody nor is it necessary for you to please everybody. It is difficult to boldly stand for God when you are concerned about what others might think or say. When you are consumed by the thoughts of others, they will control you. Worrying about what people say is dangerous because you will end up pursing what others say you should do or say instead of walking in the will of God. You will miss Gods best for your life. Your walk with God will be out of order.

In order to combat the devil you must do the same thing that Jesus did, stand firm on the Word of God. Jesus used His offense while the devil tried to put Him on the defense. When someone questions who you are, do not let your first instinct be to get defensive. Be confident in who you are in Christ. Be confident in the God in you. Sometimes the most powerful move you can make is to be still.

God has placed you in a position of power, you must choose to stand firmly in order to defeat the enemy.

The key is to STAND FIRMLY, not to stand and waver. The only way to do that is to put on the WHOLE ARMOR of God found in Ephesians 6.

I am a big football fan. My husband laughs whenever I say that because he is a Giants fan and whatever team the Giants are playing, is the team I cheer for. One of the most important strategies to winning a football game is to make sure your offensive team is intact and strong. The offensive team, is the one that drives the team to victory. God has given you the greatest offensive weapon! The Word. The word of God is mighty and powerful. It destroys strongholds. Jesus was confident in the fact that the word of God could do anything, but fail. He stood firm on what the word said and defeated the devils temptation! Forcing the devil to attempt to come with something else! When the enemy tries to get you to doubt yourself, you must do the same thing Jesus did. Stand firm in in God's word, knowing that you are who God says you are.

Philippians 4:13 teaches, you can do ALL things, not some, not a few, but ALL things through Christ. When the enemy attacks your character, your ability, your integrity STAND firm on God's word knowing that you are a child of a King and there is a King living on the inside of you!

Affirmation #5

I JOYFULLY WEAR the ARMOR of GOD!

I have the POWER TO destroy STRONGHOLDS through GODs word!

NO WEAPONS FORMED against ME SHALL PROSPER!

Chapter 6

Worthy not Worthless

Chapter 6

Worthy not Worthless

Who am I? What is my true identity? These are questions that flood the minds of many women throughout the day. If you want to see yourself through God's eyes, you have to turn to His living word. The sad reality is that too many women are walking around looking for acceptance and approval in the wrong places. When God created you, He stamped His approval on you. God's word should always have the final say in your life. Your mother and father were not your creators they were simply the vessels that God chose to use to bring you into this world. You are worthy, not worthless. Know your worth!

In order to learn your true identity, you must tap into God's word; learn what God thinks about you and the depth of His love for you.

Genesis 1:26 NLT, "Then God said, "Let us make human beings in our image, to be like us. They will reign over the fish in the sea, the birds in the sky, the livestock, all the wild animals on the earth, and the small animals that scurry along the ground.""

You were created in the image of God and given power to rule. You are a ruler! God does not focus on your shortcomings. He never focuses on your failures. That would bring the whole Kingdom down. He sees you with all of the beautiful gifts and talents that He put inside of you. He created you and to Him you are a masterpiece.

You are more valuable than gold. When He looks at you, He sees priceless gems! He sees your success, your destiny, your victory, your power, your ministry and all of the special things that He put inside of you. God wants you to discover the beauty and the wonder that's already inside of you. As a child of God, it is your duty to spread the gospel of Jesus Christ and build the Kingdom. The only way to do that is to know the power that has been placed inside of you and to know the source of that power.

The word of God in Luke 10:19 NKJV says, "Behold, I give you the authority to trample on serpents and scorpions, and over all the power of the enemy, and nothing shall by any means hurt you."

As long as you are plugged into the source, you will always walk in power and authority. Walk in your authority!

There is a great and mighty woman in the Bible by the name of Deborah, whose confidence in God, courage and prophetic anointing is immeasurable. Her vision for the world did not come from politics but it came from her unwavering confidence in God. You have to realize that in order to find your identity, you have to turn to your creator.

If you buy a product in the store and you want to find out all about the product, and the details in the making of it, you research the creator of the product, right? That is what you must do, to learn the true "you". Deborah did not have an easy assignment. She lived in a culture where men did most of the fighting and they held the leadership positions. Yet because God had a purpose for her life, she exerted enormous courage, to initiate a war on Sisera's army. In order to fulfill divine purpose, you will need to go to war. Now before you sign those military papers for the army or navy, put the pen down, that's the wrong war. The battle you will fight is a spiritual war. When God wakes you up at 3am or 5am, it is not for you to catch up on your shows. God is trying to equip you for war and build your spiritual muscles. There was no room for fear, because Deborah had faith in the word of God. She knew her identity. In order to fulfill your purpose, unleash Deborah in you.

The enemy might have an army out for you but his army calculations failed to account for one variable: the strategic power of a woman's prayer.

In Psalm 139:13-18 NLT David said:

"You made all the delicate, inner parts of my body and knit me together in my mother's womb. Thank you for making me so wonderfully complex! Your workmanship is marvelous—how well I know it. You watched me as I was being formed in utter seclusion, as I was woven together in the dark of the womb. You saw me before I was born. Every day of my life was recorded in your book. Every moment was laid out before a single day had passed. How precious are your thoughts about me, O God. They cannot be numbered! I can't even count them; they outnumber the grains of sand! And when I wake up, you are still with me!"

God loves you with an everlasting unconditional love. He is always with you.

King David was a man after Gods own heart. He was a great warrior and conquered many armies but he could not conquer, himself. He was weak in his flesh and one night of lust with Bathsheba, caused disastrous consequences in his life. His life was a roller coaster of emotional highs and lows, yet God's thoughts towards him were precious and could not be numbered. You might feel unworthy and discouraged because of the path your life has taken. Maybe you committed adultery, cheated, lied, betrayed a friend or did something that you feel in your heart you cannot be forgiven for. You might feel that you are who you are, and God cannot use you. Let me remind you that God does not look for a perfect people to build His kingdom; He looks for people that are after His heart, and have an attitude of repentance. Rahab was a prostitute and adulterer, but God used her to hide the two spies in Jericho.

People, who think they are perfect, leave no room for God to work.

People will only do unto to you what you allow them to do. Embrace self-love. Do not make excuses for people who walk over you or the men in your life who treat you with disrespect and lack of love. Do not make excuses for abuse! If you are in an abusive relationship, seek help. Reach out to someone and organizations that can help you. Do not listen to those who say you can stick it through. God did not create you to be anyone's punching bag. Do not be discouraged by the negative comments others make towards you. Don't allow your heart to become filled with anger and pain when folks write you off and discourage you. Know your value and don't accept anything less than Gods best in your life.

"Let not your heart be troubled; you believe in God, believe also in Me." John 14:1 NKJV

God always thinks lovely thoughts of you no matter what. God doesn't love you based on what you do. His love for you is UNCONDITIONAL. His plan is to give you hope and a future. Not just any future, but a bright future overflowing with many blessings.

"For I know the thoughts that I think toward you, says the Lord, thoughts of peace and not of evil, to give you a future and a hope." Jeremiah 29:11 NKJV

God wants to prosper you in every area of your life. His desire is for you to have wealth, not to be living paycheck to paycheck.

In order to walk in the promises of God, you must renew your mind in God's word and change your attitude. You might not have a million dollars in your savings account today, but you can dress, walk and stand boldly with the mind frame and attitude of a millionaire by holding on to the promises of God.

Change your mindset and you will change your life.

If God wills it, it shall be.

Deuteronomy 8:18 NKJV teaches that God has given you a covenant of wealth, and that you have the ability to get and create that wealth, because He has given you the power you need in order for you to be successful. You can reap a harvest of wealth. In order to reap that harvest you have to obey the laws of seedtime and harvest.

"While the earth remains, Seedtime and harvest, Cold and heat, Winter and summer, And day and night Shall not cease." Genesis 8:22 NKJV

If you are not tithing off the little God gives you, you cannot expect to reap a harvest of wealth. If you are not blessing others with what God has blessed you with, you cannot expect to reap an overflow of financial blessings. You serve a righteous, merciful and faithful God who wants to bless you, but you forfeit your overflow of wealth when you choose to be selfish with what God has given you. If you are the type of person that sow seeds sporadically then that's the type of harvest you will reap.

"But this I say: He who sows sparingly will also reap sparingly, and he who sows bountifully will also reap bountifully. So let each one give as he purposes in his heart, not grudgingly or of necessity; for God loves a cheerful giver. And God is able to make all grace abound toward you, that you, always having all sufficiency in all things, may have an abundance for every good work." II Corinthians 9:6-8 NKJV

In order to reap a continual and generous harvest, you must sow seeds continually and generously. You cannot afford to hold back your tithes. If your rent, mortgage, and bills are going to be late, then let them be late and believe God to provide a way, but you must tithe your ten percent; and you must sow your seeds. Believe God, to meet the needs of your family, while your seeds are being prepared for the harvest. When you rob God, you rob yourself of your blessings.

"Will a man rob God? Yet you have robbed Me! But you say, 'In what way have we robbed You?' In tithes and offerings. You are cursed with a curse, For you have robbed Me, Even this whole nation. Bring all the tithes into the storehouse, That there may be food in My house, And try Me now in this," Says the Lord of hosts, "If I will not open for you the windows of heaven And pour out for you such blessing That there will not be room enough to receive it. "And I will rebuke the devourer for your sakes, So that he will not destroy the fruit of your ground, Nor shall the vine fail to bear fruit for you in the field," Says the Lord of hosts;" Malachi 3:8-11 NKJV

The promises of God will never manifest in your life if you tithe or sow once or twice and quit because you did not get any results. You do not serve a microwave God or a genie.

There is no shortcut to your harvest. The world we live in wants everything done fast. It is important to know that everything in your life happens in seasons. I encourage you to trust God with EVERYTHING in your life. Trust God to meet your needs. Trust him to pay that overdue electric bill. Trust God to pay your car insurance. Your tithe provides resources for your home church and keeps it functioning properly. If you stop paying tithes to save money, you immediately stop trusting God and begin trusting the world. If you truly trust God, you know that God can provide all your needs even when it seems you cannot afford to tithe.

God thinks and work outside the box, He wants you to trust Him, even when things seem impossible to you. God will keep your water from being turned off even after the water company has issued a disconnection notice. I am witness to that! There have been times in my family where we didn't have sufficient funds to pay our water bill and God gave us favor with the manager who sent a technician to restore our water services without pay. You cannot tell me God won't do it, He has done that and more for my family! There is a season for sowing and a season for harvesting or reaping. Robbing God will hold back your blessings, your healing, your deliverance, your breakthrough, it will hold you back! On October 2nd 2013, I went to the hospital with severe pain in the back of my leg. The doctors ran blood work and said the results came back positive for a blood clot. I prayed to God for my healing and began to praise Him in advance for the miracle that was about to be poured out on my behalf. They ordered an ultrasound of my legs to locate the blood clot. The results from the ultrasound came back negative! There was no blood clot! My God is a healer! Robbing God will bring curses upon your life and delay your healing.

When you give to God from your heart and in truth, He will unleash blessings and miracles in your life. You cannot live in fear. Do not allow fear to keep you from being obedient to God's word.

"Give, and it will be given to you: good measure, pressed down, shaken together, and running over will be put into your bosom. For with the same measure that you use, it will be measured back to you." Luke 6:38 NKJV

The Bible teaches us to call those things that are not, into existent (Romans 4:17 NKJV). There is power in the words that you speak.

Your faith must supersede your reality in order for a true manifestation of God's word to occur.

You cannot expect a shift in the atmosphere if you are trembling in fear. You cannot expect a shift in your finances if you are not obeying Gods word. When you pray: "increase my finances, heal me, bless my family, and send me a husband". Your words, thoughts and attitudes must reflect the harvest you are seeking to reap. You cannot expect an increase in your finances if you are not tithing on the little God has blessed you with. God will not send you a husband if you are still carrying yourself with the girlfriend mentality. Are you really prepared for that very thing you have been praying to god for to be given to you? There are things you may want, God will not release them if you are not ready for them. You must learn to truly let go and let God!

Walk through your storms with confidence in God. Begin to walk in obedience to the word of God. Increase your maturity level spiritually, mentally and emotionally. It's time to grow up and get off the bottle feeding. You were designed to **MORE THAN CONQUER!**

STOP MAKING EXCUSES!

Affirmation #6

I LOVE and ACCEPT MYSELF UNCONDITIONALLY!

I AM CONFIDENT that I CAN ACHIEVE ANYTHING!

I LOVE MYSELF!

Chapter 7

Power of Obedience

Chapter 7

Power of Obedience

Years ago I decided to stop perming my hair and let it grow naturally. Not only was it a painful experience but it left me exposed and vulnerable. My reason for going natural had nothing to do with the natural movement that is happening today. God was dealing with me in a great way on unleashing my true identity. See, I wore so much weave that I forgot what I looked like without the weave. Now I know you are wondering, well how did she do her hair without looking in the mirror? Well, let me tell you, I was so deeply lost that I would wash my hair, blow dry it and lay my tracks all from guiding my hands on my head. In order for God to transform you, He must strip you of many things that are blocking you.

Sometimes, the biggest obstacle blocking you from your blessing is simply YOU.

I chose to stop wearing weaves in 2011 and for the first time, my husband saw my true identity and my real hair. I praise God that he did not scream and back away, Ha! To understand how profound that was, I must tell you that my husband and I met in 2003.

The Bible teaches in Isaiah 1:19-20 NLT, "If you will only obey me, you will have plenty to eat. But if you turn away and refuse to listen, you will be devoured by the sword of your enemies. I, the Lord, have spoken."

Disobedience will cause you to miss out on your blessings. Obeying God halfway is still disobedience. In the book of Genesis, God instructed Adam and Eve to not eat from the tree of knowledge of good and evil. Satan tempted them and they ate from the tree and disobeyed the commandment God gave them. As a result, they were banished from the Garden of Eden; pain and death were inflicted on all mankind. Women were introduced to the pain of childbirth. It was at that point that the pain through the process to fulfilling your purpose began. The blessings and purpose God has for you can only be achieved by obeying God's word and pressing through trials and tribulations. There are great rewards for being obedient to the word of God. Your breakthrough is in your obedience. Your healing is in your obedience. Your miracle is in your obedience!

Spiritual suicide occurs when you choose in your heart and soul to disobey Gods word. You forfeit your anointing, your power and blessings and choose to walk in self. You give up the things of God and choose to turn to the world. It was through halfheartedly obeying Gods word that Moses was not allowed to enter into the Promised Land. God instructed Moses in Numbers 20:8 to, "Speak to the rock before their eyes, and it will yield its water". In Numbers 20:11, Moses spoke to the rock, but also struck it with his rod. He disobeyed God's word.

You serve a gentle God. God will not come into your life and do anything you did not invite him to do. God gives you a choice, to either obey His will or disobey Him.

There are 2 important keys to obedience:
- Willingness
- Obedience must be learned

Being willing has to do with your attitude. It requires you to surrender your will to the will of God. You cannot expect to walk in your true identity while being out of the will of God. Surrendering to Gods will, unlock blessings into your life. When I yielded to the word of God, and surrendered my life to Him, I began to hear the voice of God speak to me more clearly. God began to deal with me on things and people in my life that needed to be removed.

Everyone cannot go with you to your destiny.

Sometimes there has to be a disconnection for there to be growth.

You will have to remove some things and some people from your life in order to walk into your destiny.

Evaluate your life for a moment. What or who has been holding you back from pursuing your dreams? Let go of the dead weights in your life and move forward.

The second key in regards to obedience can be found by looking at the life of our greatest role model, Jesus Christ.

Hebrews 5:8 NLT says, "Even though Jesus was God's son, he learned obedience from the things he suffered." Wait! Wait! Hold Up! Put Some Brakes On It! So you mean to tell me Jesus the Son of God learned obedience? YES! Everything that you face in your life Jesus already went through it. Remember he paid the ultimate price. He endured sacrifices that were so great that the human mind cannot begin to fathom it.

"Then the Lord said to Moses, "Behold, I will rain bread from heaven for you. And the people shall go out and gather a certain quota every day, that I may test them, whether they will walk in My law or not. And it shall be on the sixth day that they shall prepare what they bring in, and it shall be twice as much as they gather daily." Exodus 16:4-5(NKJV)

Obedience is learned through suffering.

Obedience is learned through test and trials. That situation you are faced with is not to death. Your trial is a setup from God to prepare you for your purpose and destiny. In order to learn obedience you must repent, be born again, study God's word and follow the leading of the Holy Spirit.

I'll say that again, you must FOLLOW the leading of the Holy Spirit.

I didn't say follow your mom, dad, auntie, uncle, or your third cousin twice removed. There are too many people walking around following the wrong leadership! God gave you the Holy Spirit not only to comfort you but also to guide you. God has also placed people in your life to lead you into our destiny. If you are not pressing into God's word, you will be blind to who those leaders are that God has placed over you. As a result, you will end up following the wrong people. If you are constantly in a state of depression, loss, and financial hardships, something is definitely wrong. Who is leading you?! Who have you been listening to?!

1 Samuel 15:22, 23 teaches that, obedience is far better than sacrifice. God does not want gifts or sacrifice, He wants obedience. God desires your obedience and promises that He will be your God and you will be His people.

"Thus says the Lord of hosts, the God of Israel: "Add your burnt offerings to your sacrifices and eat meat. For I did not speak to your fathers, or command them in the day that I brought them out of the land of Egypt, concerning burnt offerings or sacrifices. But this is what I commanded them, saying, 'Obey My voice, and I will be your God, and you shall be My people. And walk in all the ways that I have commanded you, that it may be well with you." Jeremiah 7:21-23(NKJV)

God created you for a specific assignment. There is a purpose for your life and a destiny for you to reach. There are people waiting to hear your story so they can be free from the hurt and pain that has kept them bound for so long. Will you not obey? If you are like me, you have a list of excuses why you are not qualified for the assignment you feel pressing on your heart. When you sit and make excuses for why you cannot go, why you cannot speak and why you cannot minister. The more excuses you make, the longer people have to wait for the testimony that would lead to their deliverance. Their deliverance is in your obedience. Always remember, God doesn't call the qualified, he qualifies the called. If God has called you, He will certainly equip you to carry out your assignment successfully. When the Angel of the Lord came to call Gideon to be the leader over the Israelite army, Gideon was the youngest of all the sons in his house and his clan was the weakest. Paul was a murderer. Sarai was barren. Rahab was a harlot. Moses was a stutterer.

Timothy was timid. Even though they might not be who the world would use to lead a generation or movement, God chose to fulfill His purposes and manifest his power through them. God can use you! Will you obey, will you say yes?

"But God has chosen the foolish things of the world to put to shame the wise, and God has chosen the weak things of the world to put to shame the things which are mighty; and the base things of the world and the things which are despised God has chosen, and the things which are not, to bring to nothing the things that are, that no flesh should glory in His presence." 1Corinthians 1:27-29

Pray:

Lord I don't know why you have chosen me to fulfill your purpose. I am not qualified but I know you have qualified me. I am not equipped for this assignment, but I know you will equip me with everything I need. Give me strength in my weakness. Replace my fears with FAITH. Give me POWER in powerlessness. I stand trusting you. I say yes to your will for my life. Amen.

Affirmation #7

I WILL obey GODs EVERY WORD!

I AM SETAPART for GREATNESS!

I will NO LONGER carry DEAD WEIGHTS!

Chapter 8

I Declare!

Chapter 8

I Declare!

Declare the Word of God Over Your Life

"Death and life are in the power of the tongue, And those who love it will eat its fruit." Proverbs 18:21 NKJV

The words you speak has the power to either build up or destroy. You may not be living in a certain experience as yet but you are to declare it and claim it over your life. You can become captive by negative words that have been spoken over your life. It is important to declare the word of God not only over yourself but over your family. It is by declaring the word of God that you draw a line to generational curses. Words of life and truth destroys strongholds and builds up your self-esteem. The word of God says, faith comes by hearing. When you speak it, you believe it. The power of God begins to manifest in your life. These are daily declarations for you to write on a sticky not and post in your common areas. Speak them over your life daily. Watch as God begins to transform your life and renew your mind.

I Declare:

- *I declare, I am the head and not the tail.*

- *I declare, I am fearfully and wonderfully made.*

- *I declare, I am not forgotten for God promised to never leave me nor forsake me.*

- *I declare, healing over my body, from the crown of my head to the sole of my feet.*

- *I declare, I have power and authority and will walk in it.*

- *I declare, I will be who God has called me to be.*

- *I declare, my voice has power to shift the atmosphere and bring forth change.*

- *I declare, any adversity, attack, accident and tragedies the enemy has set in place for me are cancelled in the mighty name of Jesus.*

- *I declare, victory over every area of my life.*

- *I declare, the spirit of anxiety has no place in my life in Jesus name.*

- *I declare, the blood of Jesus over my life, my family, my friends and everything I touch.*

- *I declare, my finances will overflow according to the will of God and I will be a blessing to many.*

- *I declare today, that I will not be defeated, discourage or depressed.*

- *I declare I shall lack no more.*

- *I declare, each member of my family, will accept the gift of salvation and become filled with the power of the Holy Spirit.*

- *I declare, anything in my life that does not line up according to the Word of God, be uprooted right now in Jesus name.*

- *I declare, every promises God has given me, shall come to pass.*

- *I declare, every situation in my life will work out for the good, according to the will of God.*

- *I declare, I will change my confessions and speak words that will bring forth growth and victory in my life and the lives of others.*

- *I declare, I will walk by faith and not by sight.*

- *I declare, from this day forward I will not be afraid to dream big dreams. I will write my visions and pursue them.*

- *I declare, I am no longer a victim but a victor. Every setback has been a setup for my comeback. My greater is coming.*

- *I declare, I am blessed in the midst of my trials and I am coming out stronger and wiser.*

- *I declare peace in my house.*

- *I declare, Satan has no power over me. I have been delivered from the power of darkness.*

- *I declare, I will stand in expectation of a manifestation of God's power and favor in my life.*

- *I declare, this is my season for Grace, favor and growth. I shall bear fruit.*

- *I declare, I will reap a great harvest from the seeds I have planted.*

- *I declare, my children will be set apart from the world. God's hand is on their lives.*

- *I declare, no weapons formed against me or my family shall prosper.*

- *I declare, I am more than a conqueror through Christ Jesus who strengthens me.*

- *I declare, I will no longer worry or doubt; I will focus on God and stand on His word.*

- *I declare, the spirit of infertility has no place in my life. I speak to my womb and declare it must line up with the Word of God and bring forth life.*

- *I declare, the weapons of my warfare are not carnal but mighty for the pulling down of strongholds and destroying yokes.*

- *I declare, I am an overcomer by the blood of Jesus and the word of my testimony.*

- *I declare, I am moving forward and letting go of my past. I am NOT going back.*

- *I declare, I am worthy and not worthless.*

- *I declare, I can do all things through Christ who strengthens me.*

Affirmation #8

THIS IS MY SEASON for FAVOR!

I WILL RISE ABOVE EVERY OPPOSITIONS!

I REFUSE to look like what I am going through!

Chapter 9

CEO of Your

Authenticity

Chapter 9

CEO of Your Authenticity

When God created you, He created you for a purpose and placed great power within you. You have to become the "CEO of Your Authenticity". Become the **Chief Empowering Officer** of your authenticity. I had to learn to stop waiting on others to come and speak life into me and my situation. I learned to empower and encourage myself. You have to want it bad enough. Whatever vision God has given you, you have to want it so bad that even if you have to drag yourself by the neck of your own shirt and say "enough is enough, get up out of this mess!", that's what you must do. Nobody can want it for you, you have to want it for yourself. You get one life to live, one chance to fulfil your purpose, it's now or never!

You must activate the power of God within you and rise above your circumstances in order to become authentic. You have to uproot every label that has been placed on you by people in the world. You must be woman enough to face the woman looking back at you in the mirror. Yes, you might have facing some difficult, painful times in your life, but you must move pass the pain to get to your purpose.

Rise above the pain and guilt from being raped, abused, molested, low self-esteem, divorce, homelessness and anything else that is keeping you cooped up in a shell. Rise above!

In order to become the CEO of Your Authenticity, you have to know who you are. Who are you? You are more than your name, you are more than your titles. You might define yourself by your race, age, gender or even title, but that is not who you are. I remember staring in my mirror one day asking myself that very question. Tears poured down my face because I had no answer. See I was raped by a cousin of mine one night while sleeping in my bed as a child and at the age of thirteen I was molested by one of my uncles. I was a victim of an abusive relationship at the age of fifteen. I suffered trauma from having a gun held to my back as I walked an entire block. I thought the shame and dirty feeling I felt was normal and acceptable. I suffered years of depression and low self-esteem. I had no sense of value for myself nor life. I tried many times to commit suicide, hoping to end the pain and torture but was unsuccessful, THANK GOD. Guilt, shame, and low self-esteem became my identity. I was unaware of the power inside of me. I was desperate to find out who I was that I turned to people. I went to school for nursing because many said I would make a great nurse. I studied business because many said I would be a great business woman. The more you search outside of yourself for your identity, the more off track you will become. My years of searching racked up student loans. I remember picking up the Bible one day and while reading the book of Genesis, I learned that I was made in the image of God according to His likeness. God placed immeasurable power within me. The scales from my eyes began to fall as I was introduced to MY TRUE IDENTITY. You are powerful! You are Armed and Dangerous! You are beautiful and worthy not by people's standards but by the standards God has designed you to be.

When you embrace those truths, you will begin to see yourself in a new light.

When you learn who you are, you become Armed and Dangerous. You become a threat to the enemy who seeks to destroy your destiny. You have the power within you to bring forth change. Stand your ground even when others don't believe in you. Do not waver in your identity. Labels have placed you in a box long enough, it's time to step out of the box! There is a voice inside of you that is yearning to break free. Being the CEO of Your Authenticity does not mean that you will never face trials and tribulations, it simply means that you will have the wisdom of knowing who you are in order to stand and live through it. Learn to hold yourself accountable for the decisions you make. Stop trying to live up to the expectations of others. Do not take on a task just because someone asked you to do it. Do it because you choose to use your gifts, time and abilities in that area with an honest effort that comes from the passions and gifts within you. Being authentic is not being someone you would like to be like, it is being who you really are!

Be authentic in every area of your life. In your business, home, school and everywhere you step foot. Today, people are hungry for something that is more genuine. Your Authenticity will transform the lives of others. If you are not authentic, you will get called out! People will sniff out fake and phony in a heartbeat.

6 Keys to being the CEO
of Your Authenticity

Be Real

Nobody likes fake and phony. Be genuine in your love and giving.

Be Consistent

Inconsistency is confusing to those around you and those following you. Consistency says that you are trustworthy.

Stay Committed and Keep your word

Don't allow yourself to become someone who can talk a good game but cannot back it up or effectively deliver on their promises. That is not a reputation you want for yourself.

Be Accountable

If you make a mistake, be humble enough to admit it. Own up and apologize before anyone else has the chance to publicly make a harsh judgment that could damage your reputation further. We are all humans so we all have flaws. Handle your mistakes with wisdom and class.

Learn when to keep quiet

It's great to share some secrets however, you do not need to have the same level of transparency with every relationship. You do not want to share your secrets or ideas with someone who will make it the next big news on Facebook, Instagram or Twitter.

Know your limits and stay in your lane

Do not step outside of your potential. Know when to say NO. Stretching yourself farther than you can handle will cause you to break. You did not get in the position you are in overnight. It took years of hiding in the backgrounds, for your authenticity to fade away. It will take time to get it back. Focus on the following key approaches which can be easily implemented into any area of your life to get you focused.

Authenticity Checklist

Define your "PERSONAL-GOALS"– what goals have you set for "YOU"? It is important to have goals for your life and personal growth.

Share your goals with excitement – Be excited about your business or ministry. People will not support you if you are not excited about what you are doing.

Maintain your true identity at all times – Do not become someone with multiple personalities. (No offence to those that suffer from mental illness) You cannot be a minister one day and a pole dancer the next.

Know when to share your ideas – Do not broadcast your business everywhere and to just anyone. There are things inside of you that might be a source of income for you.

Only share things of worth – Whatever comes out your mouth, let it have substance.

Position yourself as someone with authority and power – Be bold. Walk in power. Have class. What you put out, is what others will perceive. You might not be a millionaire now but dress and carry yourself with a millionaire mentality. Put an effort into your TOTAL presentation.

Only make promises you are able to keep – Do not promise what you cannot deliver.

Know your weakness and turn them into strengths – Work on your total growth.

Fall in love with yourself, get to know you – If you cannot love yourself, you will fall for traps. Be a person with standards.

Do not be afraid to be who you are! God created you for a purpose. There is a voice inside of you that is begging to be unleashed. It is time to unleash the REAL YOU!

Affirmation #9

MY thoughts and opinions ARE VALUABLE!

I AM a THREAT to the ENEMY!

I CAN, I WILL, I SHALL SUCCEED!

Chapter 10

Woman 2 Woman

Chapter 10

Woman 2 Woman

Are you woman enough to face yourself?

This exercise is taken from my coaching program titled "Daughters of Destiny"

Allow me to give you a brief piece of my history. I was born and raised in Belize Central America. I faced snakes, scorpions and black panthers without fear. I lived in Brooklyn New York for quite some time and rode the trains on my own at late hours of the night unafraid. Fear was not part of my vocabulary. I lived my life fearless. I remember the day a young man pulled a gun to my back and threatened to kill me if I didn't talk to him. Yet I kept walking the entire block until I reached a crowd never fearing the possibility of death. The day I faced myself in the mirror I trembled with fear and cried dreading the journey that was in front of me. I was afraid for the first time in years. I was afraid of the truth. On days that I was rebellious, my mother used to say to me, "get out, you think you're woman enough, get out." I was a woman but I wasn't woman enough to face the woman in the mirror.

Woman to woman is about you facing the woman you have become. The woman you have allowed to replace your true identity.

Exercise:

For this exercise you will need a journal.

I want you to stand in front of your mirror without makeup or weave. The reason for not wearing the makeup and weave is because I want you to face the true you.

In your journal I want you to write everything that you are feeling. What is the woman in the mirror saying to you? What pain is weighing her down?

What have you allowed yourself to get involved with knowing that it was wrong? What sins are you hiding? What labels are you carrying? What hurts are you holding on to? What has God called you to do but you are allowing fear to keep you crippled and stagnant?

Fornication? Cheater? Liar? Thief?

I want you to write everything you are hearing down into your journal. Every sin that you are carrying, write it down.

This is not a time to be proud. This is an intimate time between you, the woman in the mirror and God.

God's desire is for you to become the Queen that He designed.

Notice I didn't say remove them. If you remove a plant from the stem, it will regrow one day. You must uproot it to stop it from ever growing back. By uprooting it, you are making sure it does not grow again. People often confuse who their greatest enemy in life is. You are your greatest enemy. It is not the devil it is **YOU**.

I urge you to meditate on Psalm 27 NLT

"The Lord is my light and my salvation—so why should I be afraid? The Lord is my fortress, protecting me from danger, so why should I tremble? When evil people come to devour me, when my enemies and foes attack me, they will stumble and fall. Though a mighty army surrounds me, my heart will not be afraid. Even if I am attacked, I will remain confident. The one thing I ask of the Lord—the thing I seek most—is to live in the house of the Lord all the days of my life, delighting in the Lord's perfections and meditating in his Temple.

For he will conceal me there when troubles come; he will hide me in his sanctuary. He will place me out of reach on a high rock. Then I will hold my head high above my enemies who surround me. At his sanctuary I will offer sacrifices with shouts of joy, singing and praising the Lord with music. Hear me as I pray, O Lord. Be merciful and answer me! My heart has heard you say, "Come and talk with me." And my heart responds, "Lord, I am coming." Do not turn your back on me. Do not reject your servant in anger. You have always been my helper. Don't leave me now; don't abandon me, O God of my salvation! Even if my father and mother abandon me, the Lord will hold me close. Teach me how to live, O Lord. Lead me along the right path, for my enemies are waiting for me. Do not let me fall into their hands. For they accuse me of things I've never done; with every breath they threaten me with violence. Yet I am confident I will see the Lord's goodness while I am here in the land of the living. Wait patiently for the Lord. Be brave and courageous. Yes, wait patiently for the Lord."

God offers help for today and hope for the future. Your strength comes from God alone. Jesus died on the cross for your sins. You do not have to walk in shame and guilt. Every label that you are carrying Jesus took them with him on the cross. Today is a new day. Cast your cares and burdens on the Lord. Allow God to dwell in your heart, mind and soul and he will be the ruler of your life. Your steps are ordered and laced with peace, love and righteousness.

Do not be afraid of what people say or what they might think. God has you in the palm of His hands and you are the daughter of a KING.

I know people are talking bad about you, they talk about me too. Whenever I hear my name being dragged through the mud, I am reminded that they also talked about Jesus. They did worst things to Him, yet He loved unconditionally.

He never allowed His heart to be changed. I know that their rejection stings and you long to be accepted. Trust me, I've been there. It's hard to do right when the majority of people around you including Christians seem to encourage willful disobedience and sin as an acceptable lifestyle. We live in a time where Christians are going to the clubs, smoking, drinking and fornicating. Too many Christians are compromising in their walk. Like my sister Shanae St. Louis says, "Holiness is Cool"; we need to let the world know that Holiness is indeed cool. You cannot expect to transform the world by conforming to their ways. You are supposed to bring people up to the standards of our God, not bring God down to them. Gods plan for you is individually designed and purposed JUST for you! He loves you no matter what others say to the contrary. So what they talk about you, do not say an unkind word to or about them. Shower them in love and kindness. No matter what they do to you, bind it in earth and Heaven by crying out to God, NOT other people. They may curse you but God is going to bless you. Do not stray from His Presence but remain standing in faith!

"Behold, I am with you and will keep you wherever you go, and will bring you back to this land; for I will not leave you until I have done what I have spoken to you." Genesis 28:15 NKJV

Through every trial, you gain wisdom and strength. With every test, whether you pass or fail, you become more aware of God's mercy and grace in your life. When a woman gives birth, she goes through great pain, but has to endure pain to deliver her child. When we are in pain we beg for the pain to stop, we cry for help and medicine. You might not understand the pain and trials you are faced with but it is all part of Gods plan for you. If you TRUST HIM, your purpose will be revealed. Your trials will produce a power in you that can only be gained by PAIN. Stand strong with faith to produce the purpose and power God intends for you to have. God designed you to be able to withstand anything that may try to break you down. You are a unique design. God knows how much you are designed to handle and will never give you more than you can take. **You are not an accident, you are a divine design!** You have a purpose to fulfill. Your destiny is waiting. Stop running from the pain, embrace it and TRUST God. When everything in your life falls apart, that's when you will begin to see what you are truly made of. You will shock yourself! They expected you to die. They expected you to quit. They expected you to break. BUT God! Greater is He that is in YOU! He is EVERYTHING you need. His grace is sufficient!

Out of your trials flow your purpose.

You might not know how it will happen. Maybe you can't see a way out your situation. Maybe your dream seems impossible to accomplish without the finances. Trust God to provide. If He gave you the vision, He will give you what you need to deliver it. Stand on His word. If you fail, get up and try again. Your success depends on your ability to get up after each fall. When others cannot see your vision, keep believing God. Do not be afraid to pursue your dreams.

"Now to Him who is able to do exceedingly abundantly above all that we ask or think, according to the power that works in us," Ephesians 3:20 NKJV

When God created you, He created you with purpose and power. You are wonderfully made. Don't be pressured to be like other people in any type of way. God didn't create you like other people, there is only one you. There are things that God designed for you to do in this life. Don't live this life doing what others think you should be doing. Be free and bold to be you! Seek God and follow the steps He has ordered, they will lead you to your destiny.

Do not allow your uncertainty to cancel your opportunity.

Affirmation #10

I AM FREE to be me UNAPOLOGETICALLY!

I AM STRONG!

I AM a MIGHTY WOMAN of GOD!

Chapter 11
Your True Identity in Christ

Chapter 11

Your True Identity in Christ

Read the following scriptures to find out what God says about you. Learn the depth of His love for you.

- You are justified. Romans 3:24
- No condemnation awaits you. Romans 8:1
- You are set free from the law of sin and death. Romans 8:2
- You are sanctified and made acceptable in Jesus Christ. 1 Corinthians 1:2
- You are righteous and holy in Christ. 1 Corinthians 1:30
- You will be made alive at the resurrection. 1 Corinthians 15:22
- You are a new creation. 2 Corinthians 5:17
- You received Gods righteousness. 2 Corinthians 5:21
- You are one with Christ with all other believers. Galatians 3:28
- You are blessed with every spiritual blessing in Christ. Ephesians 1:3
- You are holy, blameless and covered with God's love. Ephesians 1:4
- You are adopted as a child of God. Ephesians 1:5, 6
- Your sins are taken away and you are forgiven. Ephesians 1:7
- You are complete in Christ. Colossians 2:10
- You will have eternal glory. 2 Timothy 2:10

- You are set free from your sinful nature. Colossians 2:11
- You are a member of Christ's body, the church. Ephesians 5:29, 30
- You can enter God's presence with freedom and confidence. Ephesians 3:12
- You share in the promise of Christ. Ephesians 3:6
- You are God's work of art. Ephesians 2:10
- You have been raised to sit with Christ in glory. Ephesians 2:6

Chapter 12

Identity Unleashed

Chapter 12

Identity Unleashed

It is important to master the art of Rocking out your Identity so when you STEP, demons must stop, drop and flee.

S.T.E.P: Stand Tall Encompassing Power.

You cannot build a platform to achieve your destiny if you are a question mark to yourself.

As a woman of God, your identity encompasses all the abundance of being a beloved child of God. You operate in a realm of abundant blessings and power. God has positioned you for power before your birth. Often times we confuse trials with failures and reasons to quit, but in God every trial is an opportunity for growth and increase. God through His love will transform you; you will be broken into beautiful.

You were created with great purpose and it is time for the true YOU to be unleashed.

In God, every trial is an opportunity for growth and increase.

"His tail drew a third of the stars of heaven and threw them to the earth. And the dragon stood before the woman who was ready to give birth, to devour her Child as soon as it was born." Revelation 12:4 NKJV

When the Lord begins to fulfill your destiny, the enemy will try and destroy it in its infancy. Giving birth in the natural and giving birth in the spiritual has many similarities. There is a time of conception, of waiting, of labor and then there is a delivery. In the natural, when a baby is born, that child is in its most delicate state of life. The baby must be held with proper care and protected from danger and predators. In the spirit, when you give birth to the promises of God for your life, your destiny is in its MOST vulnerable state. It is at this stage that the enemy seeks to destroy your destiny.

The enemy wants to destroy your destiny while it's small and helpless. You may not look threatening to the enemy now, you may even feel like a failure on the inside.

The enemy seeks to destroy you when you are at your weakest and most vulnerable stage in life. The enemy is afraid of your future and the gifts God has placed inside of you so he seeks to kill and destroy it. Always remember, the God of your destiny is stronger than the enemy of your destiny. God is with you! He is with you through every trial and every test. God is with you through your divorce, He is with you through cancer, He is with you through unemployment, and He is with you through the good and the bad. God is with you and He will deliver you!

Through every trial you endure, you possess more of the characteristics of Jesus Christ.

A woman must endure hard labor in order to give birth to a child. No matter how much she want the pain to stop, her pain is part of the birthing process. Work with the pain in your trial to produce the purpose God has for your life.

I decree and declare that as of today, the power of God has been activated in your life. You are no longer the person you used to be. You are blessed. You are delivered. You are worthy. You are More Than a Conqueror. You are the head and not the tail, above and not beneath. You will bear fruit. You are a woman on fire for God. You are sharp, bold and a chain breaker. *YOU ARE ARMED & DANGEROUS!*

Take time to focus and reflect on who God has called you to be. You get one life to live, live your best life now. Do not allow stress to occupy your day. Enjoy life's precious moments. Take time to appreciate your life and enjoy the simple things. Spend a day with yourself. If you don't learn to love yourself, you are setting a low standard for what you accept as "love". Take time to enjoy your family and friends. Read books that are uplifting and filled with wisdom. Do things that will bring growth to your life.

Be free to be who God has called you to be!

<u>Affirmation #11</u>

What GOD HAS for ME is FOR ME!

I WILL live everyday WITH PURPOSE!

I AM ARMED and DANGEROUS!

Mission...

You are "Armed and Dangerous". Your weapons are:

- God's Word
- The Armor of God
- Love
- Blood of Jesus
- Praise to silence the enemy
- Your testimony

Your mission, should you choose to accept it: Destroy the devil's identity theft camps throughout the land and empower other women through the word of God to fulfill their God given purpose in life.

Endnotes

- Page 5 definitions of crisis and identity

- Collins Dictionary http://www.collinsdictionary.com/ 2013

- Page 6. According to the Collins Dictionary the word identity is defined as "the condition or fact of being a specific person or thing; individuality". The Collins Dictionary defined the word crisis as "a turning point in the course of anything; decisive or crucial time, stage, or event".

- Page 6 quote

- Chapter 5 Put on the "Complete" Full Armor of God. Complete was added to make emphasis.

- Alexander Hamilton "He who stands for nothing will fall for anything

Bibliography

- Definitions were taken from the Collins Dictionary http://www.collinsdictionary.com/ 2013

- Scriptures taken from the HOLY BIBLE, New King James Version®. Copyright © 1982 by Thomas Nelson, Inc. Used by permission of Tyndale House Publishers, Inc. All rights reserved.

- Scripture quotations marked (NLT) are taken from the Holy Bible, New Living Translation, copyright © 1996, 2004, 2007 by Tyndale House Foundation. Used by permission of Tyndale House Publishers, Inc., Carol Stream, Illinois 60188. All rights reserved.

- Thomas Nelsons Super Value Series Dictionary of the Bible, Herbert Lockyer, SR., Editor with F.F. Bruce and R.K. Harrison, 1997

The Chain Breaker

Author, Biblical Counselor, Missionary, Teacher, Wife and Friend. A force to be reckoned with. She is a CHAIN BREAKER appointed by God, to break generational curses and every yoke of bondage that are keeping the children of God bound around the world.

Shermaine Reed encourages others to be bold, courageous and dream big dreams. When asked where her passion and drive comes from, she stated, "I was lost and broken at one point. I was the woman afraid to look at herself in the mirror because of the guilt and shame. I've been the cheater, liar, promiscuous woman, the low down and dirty woman all dressed up on the outside but wounded and lost on the inside. I've been that and done that! I searched for love in places many wouldn't dare go. I remember the day God called me to my purpose, I made up a name for myself, Moselina. I gave God so many excuses, I just knew He was coming down to smack me upside my head. God did a complete transformation in my life and that's why I am standing strong today. See when you learn who you are and whose you are, the chains will begin to break and your identity and posture will change!"

Born in Dangriga, Belize to parents Martha and Colin Nicholas, for Shermaine life has been a journey filled with pain, laughter and growth. Her testimony and unwavering faith did not come without a cost.

At a very young age, she became a victim of rape and molestation. The memory of her grandfather being asked by a villager to purchase her by trading cattle tormented her mind for years. It is through the power of God that transformed her life and delivered her from depression, rejection, identity crisis, oppression, low self-esteem and fear of death that she is able to accept the assignment God has birth in her. Every test in her life has become a powerful testimony that she uses to empower other women. She stands on the word of God and is a Proverbs 31 woman in the making.

Shermaine Reed lives in Virginia Beach with her husband and four children. Through Shermaine's networks, her passion for writing/music and ministering to those in need of help is evident in her daily life. She is a member of More Than Conquerors Church in Virginia Beach where she sings on the Voices of Victory praise team. She is a Youth leader, Assistant Bible College Professor and Church school teacher.

Shermaine Reed is the founder of Shermaine Reed International Ministries, which exist to spread the gospel of Jesus Christ to those that are forgotten. She travels to Toledo District, Belize to empower women and children. She graduated with a Bachelor's Degree in Biblical Studies and a Master's Degree in Christian Counseling. Shermaine is an active member of the Federal Association of Christian Counselors and Therapist (FACCT). She is currently pursuing her PhD in Christian Counseling. She is a woman on fire for God.

Closing Words

Thank you for taking the time out your day to take this journey with me and discovering who you are. I pray that you have found encouragement, hope and inspiration through this book. I encourage you to purchase More Than a Conqueror in order to build your faith in God even in the midst of your greatest storm. You have the power within you to overcome the enemy and bring forth change. I pray that a generational shift will occur in your family and starting now, power and salvation shall reign throughout your bloodline. I would like to hear from you. Please write to ssriministries@gmail.com. Until next time, my love and prayers are with you and your family. Be free to be who God has called you to be. **UNAPOLOGETICALLY!**

Be blessed,

Shermaine Reed

Stay Connected with Shermaine

Connect with Shermaine through these social media channels, and receive daily inspirational teachings and words of empowerment.

Shermaine Reed:

ssriministries@gmail.com

www.shermainereed.org

www.twitter.com/shermainereed

Instagram: srbreakingchains

Facebook Shermaine Reed International Ministries

Other Books by Shermaine Reed:

- More Than a Conqueror
  - o Available on Amazon.com ISBN-13: 978-1453514061

Prayer of Salvation

If you would like to receive all that God has promised for you and the precious gift Jesus has for you and make Him your Lord and Savior, pray this prayer:

Lord, I am a sinner. I have done many things in my life that don't please you. I am sorry and I repent for every sin that I have committed. I ask you to forgive me. I believe that you died on the cross for me, to save me. You did what I could not do for myself. I know now that my life is not my own so I give it to you. I believe you died on the cross for my sins and rose from the dead with all power in your hand. I believe that you sit at the right hand of God, interceding for me. I believe that because you died on Calvary, I now have eternal life. Help me to live every day in a way that pleases you. I love you, Lord, and I thank you that I will spend all eternity with you. Amen.

If you prayed this prayer or have a testimony to share from reading this book, please send us an email at ssriministries@gmail.com

You are now

Armed & Dangerous!

God bless you!